LESSONS FROM THE HIGHWAY OF LIFE

EDDIE JOLLEY

Thanks for being a friend Laura you to Jeff

Eddie Jolley

©Eddie Jolley 2017

Edited by Laura Allen

LESSONS FROM THE HIGHWAY OF LIFE

EDDIE JOLLEY

Edited by Laura Allen

Cover photo of Eddie Jolley by Kimberly Bryant

ISBN: 1979502668

ISBN13: 9781979502665

Dedication

Dedicated to my beautiful wife, Becky, with much love and respect.

Photograph by Faye Hamrick.

Contents

Contents

Foreword..5

Bikers...7

Family..19

Friends..37

God...43

Life Lessons 57

Relationships..91

Foreword

I don't remember exactly when I met Eddie Jolley. He was friends with my husband, Champ Allen, from the time they were Youngbloods (one of Eddie's well-known terms of endearment), until Champ died on May 14, 2017. Champ talked with Eddie on the phone the day before he died, and I know it would have made Champ happy that Eddie spoke at his funeral.

Sometime along the way, Eddie and I became friends on Facebook (hereafter abbreviated as FB). As soon as I started reading his posts, I told Champ "If Eddie Jolley was a preacher, I'd be attending his church." I don't darken the doorway of a church very often, but it was a sincere statement. He has a powerful message to share, of love and respect. In fact, he signs most of his FB posts *ML&R*—much love and respect.

I've seen many people on FB tell Eddie he should write a book. I agreed, and I have a little experience in that area, so I twisted his arm to let me help him get his message out there. It's a bit of free advice from an elder biker who has been riding more than 50 years, lived through every twist and turn in the road, done wrong and done right, loved and lost and loved again, made friends, lost friends, raised his family, learned a lot along the way, and is still humble about it. Eddie's description of himself on his FB page is "Just a Nobody trying to be Somebody."

I decided to use this post as the opening for this book:

I had a person at car show yesterday tell me that she had read some of my posts on FB and couldn't believe it was the same person she use to know...Listen up Guys, I never mean to preach or judge anyone, I'm Eddie Jolley and with the mistakes I've made in my life I couldn't if I wanted to. I post things I learned hoping I can save just one person the trouble and heartache me or some of my friends have gone through. Sometimes life is not just all about you; consider others and the heartbreak your actions can bring to them. Always love your family, take care of your friends ,and show others the respect you want in return . Know there comes a time when you just can't make it on your own and when you get to that point...Look Up.

It was my honor and privilege to help Eddie with this book. If even one sentence here speaks to you and helps you somewhere along your way, then his intention has been fulfilled.

Laura Allen

Bikers

I keep seeing "The Biker's Code," the rules for being a biker. Must have been some yuppie's way of getting on Facebook. I've run this road for over 50 years and reading someone's rules will never make you a biker; it comes from what you're made of, what's in your heart, how you treat people, or how you don't let them treat you. It's about being your own man, taking care of your brothers no matter what comes their way. It's about being you, being real, dressing the way you want, riding what you like, never following the crowd, always showing respect 'til it's not given in return...I care about everyone that rides, but hanging off the side of your bike waving isn't a rule...Be yourself, that's the good part, that's why we're bikers, we're different. ML&R

We were Bikers before Bikers were cool...started 50 + years ago. Fred "Dago" Williams, Champ Allen, and Eddie Jolley. Photograph by Samantha Beam.

There are a lot of fake bikers, but you'll never find a
biker that is fake.

Some people like to put down bikers, but I've never
seen 200 BMW'S in a roll taking toys to needy children.

People spend hours cleaning their bikes only to be one
of a hundred riding a shinny Harley. Work on the rider,
it's the man that gets off it that people will remember.

All of you know I love bikers, and what I saw today
brought a smile to my face but let me throw this at
you...anytime you're at a ride and it starts to pull out
and you see a club trying to get in line, give them your
respect, let them stay together. They came as one; let
them ride as one. Always respect the patch and it'll
respect you. It's not about who gets out first, it's about
the reason.

We buried a Brother today, not the kind that comes
from blood, but one that spent maybe a year earning
the right to belong. He belonged to an MC, but he was
also a father, son and grandpa. His hair might have been
a little too long, even a few tattoos, but a heart of pure

gold. I'm sure as the hearse went by with dozens of patched out bikers riding in the rear, they were judged by many, but what you should have done was say a prayer for them, They're laying one of their own to rest.

Too often they get a bad rap, but not many tell of the good they do. The boys down South are delivering supplies today to the flood victims in the Low Country, some are up North on a cancer run. These guys are the real deal, fists of Iron and hearts bigger than life. I like to say I'm just a nomad because I have friends that I would take a bullet for on many sides.. I show them respect and get it in return. Next time you see a patched-out biker roll by, just remember he may be a free spirit but he lives and dies just like you; all any of them want is respect. Give it to them and don't be surprised when they give it back...RIP Little Man, the circle has been broken, but one day it will come full circle again. Maybe that's why they wrote the song *Ghost Riders in the Sky*. ML&R

Sometimes I get on here and maybe spill too much of my guts, but I found out very late in life that having a heart can sometimes blow your mind. Being hard-hearted was a breeze; I saw things, but too often I was blind. You see, the Devil has a way of putting blinders on you; all you see is straight ahead and not the things around you...I met this guy just a few year ago, and I remember him telling me how he once had a bike and how he lost it...me being the butt I used to be, I kinda blew him off as a wannabe.

Somehow our paths kept crossing and we started having talks. He had His demons and I had mine. I had something happen that made me start seeing the light, thinking I needed to change a few of my ways, and as we talked, I found he was going through the same thing.

Eventually he bought a Harley. He was in the wind again, a dream had come true. He made friends with several of the guys around here. He was accepted, even if we did sometimes give him a hard time, always in fun...I didn't get to ride with him as much as I wish I had, but I'll never forget a couple of year ago I said something about going to a bike rally at the Circle J, and he asked "Can I ride with you?" He and I rode in and as soon as he got off, he came to me and said, "Thanks, you made me feel like somebody."

A man that raised his kids alone, even though he wasn't able to work, had beat his demons and he felt like somebody because he rode with me. Well, I just left this *Somebody*. He is sick, really sick. I saw a man that I almost didn't recognize. I saw his daughters taking care of him and every so often, kissing His forehead and saying " I love you, Daddy." We talked for awhile, and as I was leaving, we looked at each other, both with tears in our eyes. He said "I love you, Brother" I told him the same. Yeah, Terry Dixon, I called you my brother, and I meant it. You earned my respect, and like I told you as I headed to the door, we'll ride together again, if not down here, we'll do it up there.

When you hit your knees tonight, keep Terry and the Dixon family in Your prayers. He's fighting a battle that only God can help. ML&R Bro Man.

I talk a lot about motorcycles because they've been a big part of my life. Everyday I read where people are having problems; we all do, but life and motorcycles have a lot in common. You get on your bike, running down the highway, you've got the world by the tail, but all of a sudden, you look ahead, a black cloud is on the horizon, you feel the temperature drop, you're headed into a storm...things get dark, rain pouring down, you look around, no shelter.

You can pull over and sit there, bet your life you'll get soaked, or maybe even struck by lightning, or you keep moving, maybe at a slower speed, but you don't stop because you know in the back of your mind, "I'm gonna run out of this, maybe a mile down the road, maybe 5 but I will get through it." Listen up, guys. if you ride you'll get wet; if you've been born you're going to go through a storm. Don't ever quit, keep plugging along. No storm lasts forever. The sun may be out just over the next hill...It's call *Riding The Storm Out*. ML&R

We try to sleep, but life hits us in the gut at times, memories rush in, and tears and smiles cover my face. Late 80's or early 90's, me and a couple of friends rode into a place in Lake Lure called Margaritagrill. As I started to get off my bike, a dude pulled up and parked beside me. He was riding the dirtiest, greasiest, oil-leaking shovelhead I had ever seen, and to beat that, he had on army boots and was wearing a kilt. Me being the smartass I was back then, I looked at him and said 'long ways from Scotland." He looked at me and said "how would a redneck like you know where Scotland is anyway?" We stared for a second and then he smiles and says, "I'm Steve, let's get a beer."

Well, that's been over 20 years ago. I was there when he and Kelly got married, and she gave him a brand new Harley that I don't think he ever washed again. He wasn't the kind that washed his bike 2 hours to ride 15 minutes; he was a biker. He rode not to impress anyone, but because he loved the freedom, and the crazy thing about it was there was a bird named Sabrina that rode with him. She would draw people to him, and his personality would keep them coming back. He and I were friends, even though I had never been to his house or he to mine, but every time we met, He would hug Becky, then throw his arm around me, and and always say while making sure Becky heard him, "You don't deserve that, Bro." I don't, Bro Man, and I didn't deserve to know a man like you, Not many impress me. You did, you were the real deal. Sometimes, I look at the Youngbloods and think, "someday they'll fill our shoes, but it will take a special person to fill yours...Gonna miss you, Bro Man. Lake Lure and LBCC will never be the same without you...RIP Steve, thanks for the smiles you put on everyone's face. ML&R, this time from my heart.

Christmas will be here before you know it, and toy runs will be happening most every weekend. Over the years, I've noticed that it's usually the same people at these events giving, giving, giving, not because they have to, but because they have a heart for the kids. Listen up: Some of you ride bikes; you want to be one of us, but you never attend. There's more to being accepted than just buying a Harley and wearing the clothes.

We're a Band of Brothers, we take care of our own, but we're there for others along the way. To the guy that told me today " there's too many Clubs at those things," listen to me, Bozo, if it wasn't for the different Clubs, there would be some sad kids at Christmas. They turn out in numbers and have earned my respect...wish I could say to same about you. By the way, you don't have to ride a bike to attend; throw a toy in the car and come on out, I promise you'll see more love than you've seen in awhile.. ML&R

Returning from SC yesterday, I noticed we were going kinda slow, pulling out to see why, I saw a moped

several cars ahead. Seems like each car that passed blew their horn or made a hand gesture as they went by. Riding behind the guy, I could see him so close to the edge of the road trying to get out of everyone's way that he often hit the dirt...thinking *he's gonna get hit*, I pulled the chopper beside him; now there's two of us slowing traffic, but no longer getting a bird shot at us as they passed.

Riding side by side at 40 mph for several miles, he keeps looking over at me, at first with fear on his face, but soon with a smile. When he stopped at a gas station, I stopped with him. As he takes off his ragged old helmet, I reached out and shook his hand and said "thanks for the ride."

We talked for awhile, and I rode away thinking "I'll never look at a moped with the same eyes again."

Not everyone is a drunk...this guy had 3 kids, his wife had passed away 2 years ago, his car was broken down, and with not enough money to buy another one, this was his only means of transportation. Next time you're riding behind one of these little scooters, stay cool, maybe they are a drunk OR they could just be a Dad trying to take care of his kids. ML&R

Too much partying, unfamiliar road, three motorcycles blasting thru the night, sharp curve, a Brother is down... silent scream coming from your head, one look and you know it's too late, a wife standing with her kids at a cemetery...Guys, please be careful. I just took you through a nightmare you never want to experience. You should have seen it in color...ML&R

Stopped in at a bike rally for maybe an hour yesterday, and as I was leaving, I stopped and parked the bike at the top of the hill. As I got off and looked down in the valley at all the campers, tents, bike games going on, people having fun while raising money for a great cause, I started thinking *there's no telling how many of these things I have attended in the last 50 years*, but my body was telling me it's going to have to slow down.

There comes a time it's hard being *you*...No, there's nothing wrong with me, just reality setting in. To all you Youngbloods out there, thanks for the respect you've always showed me, and I hope I gave it back in return. Enjoy your bike, but every time you get on it, think to yourself *"this thing can kill me."* Take it easy on the bottle and run from the dope, love your family, and always take care of your Brother and Sisters; you never know when you will need them to take care of you. Let a few things go over your head; that temper can cause you a lot of trouble, and most important, there is a God and one day, you're gonna look Him in the eye. Be able to hold your head up...you'll still see the old chopper rolling through. I'm not finished yet, just slowing my roll...Guess I'm realizing I'm a has-been, but thanks to the Good Lord, I lived to say I was. ML&R

We laughed as you stumbled to your bike…"Hurry up Bro, it's getting late, we've gotta go." Up the road we flew, pipes blasting, hair flying in the wind, going into a curve way too fast…"You're down, Bro," we're screaming, "You're not breathing! God, please let this be a nightmare, wake us up, *please*!" It can happen in the blink of an eye and stick with you for a lifetime. Never let a Brother drink and ride. ML&R

Listen to those Old Bikers, you can learn alot from them. They've been down roads they hope you never travel, seen things they hope you never see. Just because you bought a Harley, you've still got alot to learn.

Sometimes a person goes through this old world thinking they're bigger than life; nothing really ever scared them, then you wake up one day and realize you're nearer to the end than you've ever been. Today as I watched nearly 200 motorcycles roll past me, doing a run for a kid in need, fear hit me. I stood in respect to each one, but my mind was racing, and to be honest with you, I guess I was a little jealous. There were a few Old Timers like me, the few who had hit a road that took us to places we shouldn't have been, made us see things that we shouldn't have seen, but mostly there were the Youngbloods, the ones that are doing it right.

16

Yeah, I saw a couple of you and I thought "there I go 30 year ago," probably not believing cow horns will hook.

I'll admit I sometimes get scared knowing that there's more days behind me than there are in front of me, but that's okay. I've been blessed I got to make it this long. Listen up, Youngbloods, don't ever get too big for your britches, The Man can rattle your cage in a heartbeat. He can bring you from a hero to a zero just that fast.

Always keep your head on straight, when that little voice you hear saying "*No*" goes away, you're in trouble; you've lost your way. Life is not about how many men you whipped, how much booze you could drink, how many women you had, and really it doesn't make much difference how big the bank account is. I'm thinking none of that is going to impress God when we hit that Big Gate in the Sky, it's all going to come down to what you had in your heart, how you treated family and friends.

As the song says, *"All we are is dust in the wind."* There's got to be something better ahead. Thanks for the respect you show me today, you sure have mine...Be Safe, Ride Free, and don't put off until tomorrow what you know you need to do today. ML&R

Image by Freddie Ray Ellis

Family

Family are those that are there for you no matter what. Blood has nothing to do with it.

God has a way of getting to you even in your sleep; memories or dreams can wake you in the middle of the night. Getting up this morning at 4 with nothing else to do, I turned on Facebook and the first thing I saw was a post my youngest son, Chad, had written about how he loved and missed His Mom. Bam! Now I not only have my Dad in my head; my ex enters my heart...two people that were such a blessing to me in my younger days when I was too stupid to realize it. The mistakes I made flooded my mind: the words I should have said, like "Thank You", "I'm sorry", "You were right", and the other words and actions you both deserved. "I love you" came so easy while on my knees in the middle of the night. I'm so sorry I couldn't get them out when You were here to hear them.

Now you're both gone to a better place, and I sit here with tears in my eyes...Just know one day I'm coming through that gate and you two will be the first ones I'll seek, because with the help of God and some good people, I've pulled myself out of the pits of Hell, the Wild Child has found his way home...RIP Renee, you left behind two well-respected sons and grandkids you would have adored. You, too, Dad, RIP. I didn't give you a lot down here. I'm sorry I didn't give you the credit you deserved, and as I look back now, you were My Hero. Pride, foolish pride just kept me from showing you...I don't know what it is but there's something about a Sunday. ML&R

After my last post, I get a message "is there anything you didn't do?" Yes...I didn't give my parents the love and respect they deserved. My Dad died, and I didn't tell him I loved him. I didn't always respect authority. I didn't always say no to the drugs and the bottle. I didn't save a Brother from dying. I didn't save my first marriage. I didn't keep a loved one out of jail. At one point, I think I didn't even believe in God...yeah, there's lots of things I didn't do; that's why I come on here and try to tell you what you need to do.

Love and respect your parents, take care of your friends, stay away from drugs, be careful with the booze, work at your marriage, warn a friend when he's doing wrong; there's rules in life, like them or not, abide by them, and most important, never stop believing that there's a God. No matter how tough, rich or stubborn you are, one day something will knock you to the ground, and you're going to need to look up and have something to believe in. There are too many things I didn't do, but when I leave this world the Man Upstairs can't say " You didn't try to warn them." ML&R

The best part of life is when your family become your friends and your friends become your family.

Kinda funny how when your Dad was living, you didn't need his advice, but when he's gone, there's a hundred questions you'd love to ask. ML&R

Always pay attention to your parents; it's better to be criticized by someone that cares than to be praised by a gang of fools.

Dads, if you have a small son just starting to play football, lighten up a little, encourage them, don't scream at them. These are just kids trying to make you proud. Don't try to make them something You never were. ML&R

No parent, child or family is immune to drugs. Be careful when talking about another. ML&R

The moment you start putting your happiness before your kid is the day you cease being a parent.

"The most important thing a father can do for his children is love their mother."

~ Theodore Hesburgh

Stop turning your head when your kids do wrong, hold them accountable for their actions. If not, you're creating the assholes of tomorrow. ML&R

If you tell a kid you're going to do something, do it. They'll find out the world is full of liars soon enough; you don't want to be the one that gave them their first lesson. ML&R

I was told from an early age if I did wrong, "God's gonna get you for that," and every time something bad happened, I'd think "Okay, You got me. "...almost got to the point it was me against Him. That's not the way it works. I finally found out He was on my side all the time. Parents, I know you mean well, but be careful what you say to kids; they take it to heart.

Putting the kids first: The best gift divorced parents can give their children this holiday season...don't be fighting over the kids, this is their time of the year...let them enjoy it. ML&R

22

Spending time with your child is more important than the money you hand them. It's better to be remembered as a loving parent than a walking ATM machine. ML&R

Don't be the parent that raises hell with your teenager during the day and pray they get home safe that night. ML&R

You don't have to be rich to be a good parent. When your child grows up, he'll remember you playing catch with him, not how much you paid for the ball. ML&R

If you knew today would be your last, would you call and tell your loved ones how much you loved them? I'm betting you'd find the time to go by and see them...most of us would fall on our knees and beg God to forgive our sins. Think about it: On September 11, 2001, hundreds of people woke up, dressed and walked out their door thinking they'd be in their bed that night. It never happened. Live everyday like it's your last...we never know when our world will stop turning. ML&R

There comes a time in every parent's life when you have to realize your child is an adult. They're married with

kids of their own; being a good parent means controlling yourself and stop controlling your kid. You love them enough to do anything for them, now let them be themselves.

One day you're going to miss those phone calls and text messages; you're going to miss how they worried about you when you were out too late; you're going to miss how it feels to have someone on their knees praying for your safety; you're going to miss having someone that loves you no matter what...yeah, one day you're going to miss your parents. ML&R

Rode down to my old home place yesterday. Kinda funny how a gloomy Saturday can bring back so many memories...As I sat in the car with *"Against the Wind"* playing on the CD, a smile came to my face as I remembered the Sunday lunches, the Christmas gatherings, the kids and grandkids playing in the yard, but as I walked around, the tears started choking me from inside...I thought of the times I worried Mom and Dad, not seeing them for days, the fussing and fights that had gone on in that yard, the prayers that had been sent through the roof of their bedroom late at night for a boy lost in sin. Somehow God saw fit for me to live to return yesterday. The place stands silent now; Dad has been gone for years and Mom is not doing good; it's just a house on a lonely hill.

The place I couldn't wait to get away from is now is the place I'd give my right arm to be able to go back to. The things I didn't say then would be the first thing out of my mouth today. I remember Dad once telling me, *"maybe you'll find what you're looking for someday."* After so many mistakes, wrong roads traveled, and a lifetime behind me, I think I found it yesterday, Dad...it was right here under my nose all the time. ML&R

While some kids go back to school and talk about their vacation, some will remember working at McDonald's. While some laugh about the party they had last night, others will remember seeing their parents laid out on drugs. While some remember having fun on a date, others remember taking care of that little brother or sister. While some get in their new car, some will be looking out the window of the bus only wishing. God created us all equal but some just travel a rougher road. Teach your kids to always hold their head high but not so high they can't see the ones below. ML&R

When schools is getting ready to start a new year, please tell your kids that there will be a little girl there that may not have on the latest fashion clothes, or a boy that didn't get the new Nike shoes that he had wished for. Some of these kids are just lucky to have a

bed and something to eat. Poor kids aren't usually very popular, friends are hard to come by; just a cheerleader or a football player speaking to them could change their whole school year. If your kid is a Somebody, please encourage them to make someone else a Somebody this year as well...It'll be one of the best lessons they'll learn all year...thanks. ML&R

You can buy your kids fancy clothes, the nicest toys, even give them a great education, but you know just how rich you are when they run to your arms when your hands are empty.

Waking up to a house alone has a way of taking you back in time, a place you should have never gone. Thinking of how you had killed the love of the ones you didn't think was possible, finding yourself in a world alone, running a road without a clue. The Sunday mornings you awake feeling like a zero even though last night you thought you were a hero. Driving from someone's house that this time yesterday was a total stranger, on the way home you pass a church and see families walking through the door, or pass a house and see kids playing in the yard, and your mind drifts back and the smile on your face turns into a tear in your eye. You pull into your driveway and walk through the door only to realize how big and quiet it is when everyone is

26

gone. You shower, change clothes, but somehow the walls close in, you start to realize you no longer like your own company so you're off running, trying to find some kind of peace, some kind of meaning in life, the very thing you had and didn't have enough sense to keep.

I told you that to say this: work on your marriage, never take a person's love for granted, anything can be ·killed...don't find yourself one day searching for what you once had and threw away. Hurry home Becky, Sunday morning is coming down. ML&R

I sit here at this moment one if the biggest hypocrites on Facebook. I put up a post this morning telling you to tell Loved Ones how you feel before it's too late, knowing I had an ex-brother-in-law in the hospital not doing very well. I had put it off but had every intention of going down tonight. My son Chris just called and said Terry passed away a few mins ago. I blew it, guys. I'm just an Old Fool that has kneeled at way too many tombstones and said "I'm sorry." The bad thing about is it never spoke back and said "it's ok." RIP, Terry Allen.

Today I stopped by my Dad's. We sat on the porch and talked for hours. I told him how much I appreciated everything he had done for me, told him I was sorry for all the worry and pain I had caused him, thanked him for loving my mom, his kids and grandkids, even looked

Him in the eye and told him, "I love you, Dad." Only wishful thinking for me...if you still have a Dad, you still have the chance...if only I could turn back the Hands of Time. ML&R

I heard a kid disrespect his stepdad yesterday by saying "You're not my real dad." Me knowing the situation wanted to say "Li'l Brother, this man came into your mother's life and loved her enough to accept and raise you as his own while your real dad ran like the lowlife he is." Step-parents should be some of the most respected people around, they walked up to the plate as a pinch hitter while the real player sat on the bench. ML&R

Parents spend so much time working just to give their kids what they didn't have, that they cheat them out of what they did have....a family. Too many kids growing up homeless while living in the family house. Wake up, you only have them for a short time. ML&R

You may think your kids aren't listening when you talk, but you can bet they're watching what you do. ML&R

Sometimes people say that they have no regrets in life, and I figure they must have never lived, and thinking we'd all do things differently if we had another chance.

My Dad died several years ago, but had he lived, today would have been his birthday. He was a good man, always worked hard to provide for his family, took us to church, fought for his country...old school as they come, always telling me "if you live in my house, you go by my rules," and it seemed like I was a hardheaded rule breaker.

I know I gave him some happiness, but I caused a lot of heartbreak and worry; he didn't give up on me even when I thought it was more fun running with the Devil than walking with God...Youngbloods, if you still have a Dad, spend some time with him, listen to what he has to say...one day you'll see he wasn't as dumb as you thought. Thank him for all he did for you, and never be too macho to tell him you love him. I can tell you from experience when he's on his deathbed, the words will come easy, but you know you've waited too late, you blew it. Happy Birthday in Heaven, Dad. I finally figured out I'm not 10 feet tall and bulletproof...Life beat me to my knees but when I was there I got things right. Some day we'll talk again, but 'til then, RIP, RD Jolley...ML&R I give you.

Tomorrow I'll spend some time with my kids. Tomorrow I'll tell my spouse "I love You." Tomorrow I'll call up my parents and just say hello. Tomorrow I'll get right with God...Maybe you should think about it TODAY just in case tomorrow falls through. ML&R

Never give up on your kid, God had the Only Perfect Child...

As some of you know, my Mom is in her 90's and due to health problems, she's having to spend the rest of her life in a nursing home. I went to visit her yesterday and though her hearing is almost gone, and she doesn't say a lot anymore, sometimes I just look at her sitting in that wheelchair and wonder what's going on in her head. She's in her own little world, out-lived most of her friends, and seems to be forgotten by the rest.

As I start to leave, I kiss her on her forehead and tell her "I love you, Mom." Tears come to her eyes and she looks at me and asks, "Do You ever go to your Dad's grave?" I shook my head yes, even though I was lying. She smiled and said, "You know, he really did love you." We waved goodbye, and as I got in my car I knew where I had to go...I went to visit Dad. As I cleared the grass from his grave marker and read the words written, a lump came up in my throat as I thought how hard he worked to raise a family, the things he did without so we could have more, the mornings he went to work with no sleep because he was up all night worrying about me, where I was, if I was OK. The one man that always had my back even when I was wrong, was in my mind at times my worst enemy.

What a fool I was, and as I sat beside his grave, I told him just that...kinda doubt if he heard it, should have told him while he was alive but that's something I have to live with. Today Is Labor Day, maybe it's not about us, but the ones before us that worked their butts off raising a family. If your parents are living today and you're off, maybe you should go see or call them and just say "Thanks." It's hard to tell them when they're 6 feet under. ML&R

Paid Mom a visit at the nursing home today. While pushing her outside she spotted my bike. She looked at me and said "You were living too fast. God took care of you. You know I prayed for you everyday." As I kissed her on the cheek and said "I know, and thanks," the thought ran through my mind, *"Who's gonna pray for me when Mama's gone?"* Never stop praying for your kids, it takes some longer than others. ML&R

As most of you know, Mom has been in a nursing home for the past couple of years, but the last 6 months have been an emotional roller coaster...watching your hero slowly slip away is an ordeal that will melt the hardest heart.

As I watch her sleep and listen to her rattling cough, I can't help but think of the Sunday lunches, the family gathering for Christmas, how she helped raise my kids and loved her grands and great-grands. How she worked 10-hour days and still had the time to do the cooking, washing and cleaning, and still smile and show me and my sister love. I think of the times I made her smile, but I also think of the hell I put her through, the times I broke her heart ,and how at my worst, she never stopped loving me....she was never ashamed to tell people *"that's my boy."*

Now she's in a strange place, the visitors have stopped, her hearing is gone. As she sleeps, I kiss her cheek and she opens her eyes and says "Eddie," and reaches for my hand. I know in my heart She is saying " I love you," fighting back the tears, all I can do is nod my head and say "I love You too." As I write her a note and say "I'll see you tomorrow," and get ready to walk out the door, I always wonder if I will I see her again, or is this going to be the last time. I guess only God knows that answer, but you can bet your life instead of walking away with her still talking like I did so many times, I pause at the door and pray. I could hear her say "Everything is going to be alright," just one more time. Love and respect your Mama. They're special gifts sent to you from Heaven. Goodnight, Mom. ML&R

Mom went to Heaven on 02/09/2017.

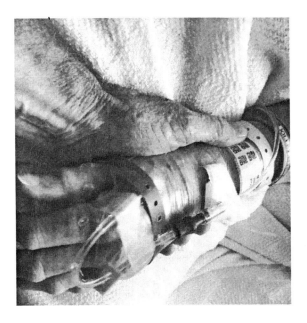

When our kids were small and I'd ask Mom to babysit, more than once she reminded me, "Your Dad and I never went anywhere that we couldn't take our kids." Might have been one of the reasons they were married for 63 years...just thinkin'.

Don't bring that stranger home for the night if the kids are there. You may not respect yourself, but at least respect your kids.

Never get a *house* and a *home* confused...there's lots of houses still standing while the home has crumbled. You

do the upkeep on your house, do it on your home.
ML&R

Never talk bad about another person's child, one day
you may need their advice on how they got through it.
ML&R

Watching all the protesting and rioting going on today
makes one think instead of leaving a better world for
our kids, maybe we should have left better kids for our
world. ML&R

There comes a time in each parent's life when the only
dreams they have are that their kid's dreams come true.
ML&R

Sometime a song can bring back so many memories.
God gave me a good life, I just brought some bad things
into it...looking back I took so many wrong roads, but
gosh, it was my life, why would Mom and Dad try to tell
me how to live it? In my old age I figured it out; you see,
if we went through life alone, that's one thing, but there
are people out there that love us, and when we screw
up and divorce, they go through the pain. When we are

high on drugs and the bottle, we drag them into the gutter with us. When we go to jail, guess who is sitting beside us? It's the people that loved and believed in us. Yeah, it was our life but our loved ones, even though they didn't ask for it, took the ride with us.

Youngbloods, you still have time, look around and if you're hurting the people you love, change it. it's not always "about you"...oh yeah, the name of the song was *"Funny how time slips away"*. ML&R

How many storms in life could have been avoided if we had just listened to Mama?

You can work your butt off to give your kids the best of everything, but you can make or break them with your words. ML&R

Every kid deserves a childhood; too many are having to grow up too fast because their parents won't.

Everyone wants more in life...that means more work, more stress, more time away from family. Why not have less? That means less work, less stress, and less time away from family....Sometimes LESS is MORE.

I got up early this morning and went to visit my Dad...told him how much I loved him and how I appreciated every thing he had done for me...I knelt down in front of him and apologized for the hell I put him through, for all the times I broke his heart. My Mom was there with him this year, so she got to hear it too. Listen up, Youngbloods, I was talking to a stone; if you still have your parents let them know you love them, not just today but everyday. Don't be caught walking away looking over you shoulder thinking *"what I'd give for just one more day."* Happy Fathers Day, my friends. ML&R

Friends

Talked to a man today that many years ago ran a small junkyard. I asked him if he remembered picking up a certain car back in 1967...he kinda laughed and said NOPE...I knew he picked it up that night, so he told me I was free to go by his old place and see, as a lot of the old cars were still there. The more I thought about it, the more I knew I had to go look.

Walking through the weeds, dodging briars and watching for snakes, I spotted it...there hidden by time was a 1967 Chevelle SS, no longer black on black, with a 396ci 4 speed. I remember that car when it was new, as I walked around a rolled up piece of rusty steel, I remembered the night my buddy and I sat at a little country store and talked, just 2 guys, 2 Chevelle SS's, radio playing on a summer night, sitting window to window, shooting the breeze, making plans for tomorrow night. "Talk to you tomorrow!" I said, and pulled out sideways with him on my bumper. I went home, that night I pray he went to Heaven...they say he hit a tree running better than 100 mph. Tomorrow never came...*Why* is a big word, God, but someday I gotta ask You...

When your friends are going through a storm, you can be either a power outage or a rainbow.

A fake may change friends, but friends can't change a fake. ML&R

I don't know if this year is special, or I've just slowed down enough to look around, but people, we have friends out there that are hurting. We've got to stick together and help each other through this world...just an old fool thinkin' out loud...

They say "You are what your friends are." Mine are rich, poor, young, old, white, black, smart, not-too-smart, male, female, good, bad... I'm confused, who am I?

A brother is not always a friend, but a friend is always a brother.

Fake friends are like a shadow: always near you at your brightest moment, but nowhere to be seen at your darkest hour!

Want to realize the value of a friend or family member? Lose one...

The enemies you make by taking a stand generally have more respect for you than the friends you make by sitting on the fence.

If you have to kiss someone's butt to be their friend, tell them to jerk those drawers up and hit the highway! ML&R

Think back to your childhood; other than your parents, was there a man or woman that you looked up to and was an influence on your life? You may not know it, but there's someone looking up to you right now...don't let them down. ML&R

Be there for people when they're going through a loss. Maybe it's a relationship, a job, or even a loved one's passing...Never think "it's not that bad." God could show you it *is*...First-Hand. ML&R

Don't go through life carrying a grudge. Not speaking to family or friends will one day come back and bite you...they call it a funeral. ML&R

We call on our friends in the good times, " let's go ride, let's go eat" because we want to be with them. We want to laugh with our friends, but why do we hesitate to call them in the bad times? Are we afraid we'll be judged, talked about, or maybe just afraid we'll lose their friendship? When you have true friends, you can lay your life in their hands; you trust and know, no matter what, they're there with you, to hold you up in the bad times...thinkin' we all should strive to be this kind of friend.

I've been accused of a lot of things but heard a new one today: "Eddie, you work the crowd." Listen up, I probably spoke to or hugged no less than 100 people this weekend. You may call it work; I call it *loving life*. Never let it be a hardship to love a Brother or Sister. ML&R

Friends aren't jumper cables, you don't throw them into the trunk and pull them out for emergencies.

You don't need a certain number of friends, just a number of friends you can be certain of. ML&R

While coming through Spindale yesterday, I glanced over at several men standing in a motel parking lot. "RED FLAG"...A little ways down the road, I thought to myself, "I know one of those guys." As I turned around and drove back into the parking lot he saw me and started to walk away. I followed him into his room. The place was a mess, he was a mess.

This guy was part of my past, hadn't seen him in years...a man that once had a good job, a beautiful wife, and a great kid was now homeless, sores on his face, teeth missing, everything he had dreamed of in life GONE...all because of a party when someone pulled out the meth pipe and he said "Why not, just one time." He said he could never lay it down, always searching for more. Life shot in the azz, wife and kid now history, old friends forgotten, new friend: METH.

Youngbloods, Meth is Death! It'll eat your mind and body, but worse yet, it eats your soul. I'm not much at fighting anymore and wouldn't advise you to, but if someone hands you a pipe and says "try it," knock it down their throat. I'll go your bond...Have a great day and always live it so you can remember It. ML&R

People are going to come into your life, but if you live long enough, you will watch them leave...I wish I could tell you it gets easier, but that would be a lie. My Dad once told me " Boy, the longer you live, the more friends you will bury." To my Youngbloods who feel like their guts have been ripped out, cry, scream if you must, then let it go. Remember the good times, and always know it's better to die while living than to live while dying. Don't cry because they're gone; smile because you had the chance to meet them.

Life is just what it is. You can't hide from heartbreak, it hits us all at some point, and there's no hiding. Look around at family and friends, let them know you love them just in case tomorrow they are gone, you can look back and think "I could have missed the pain but I'd have had to miss the dance...Thank God we danced. Love you, Youngbloods, ML&R always.

God

While talking to a very special Youngblood today, I was trying to warn him about life when he looked at me and said, "I'm still young, what were you doing at my age?" As I looked at him with his long hair, tattoos, invincible attitude, I almost saw myself at that age...always looking for a good time but seeing too many of them go bad. We had a ball running with our buddies but lived a nightmare as we walked them to their graves. The booze flowing tonight while the tears were flowing the next morning when you heard one didn't make it home...the dope making you fly like an eagle while turning some into jailbirds...listening to Dad raise hell before you walked out the door but not seeing him and your Mom on their knees that night begging God to spare you one more time.

Yeah, Kid, I'm old now, I just want to see you do better than me. Have fun but know that in 5 seconds, your whole world can change. Always believe in The Man because if you live to be my age, He's the one that got you there. ML&R

Saying "There's no hope" for someone is like saying "There's No God". ML&R

Most of us pray, usually about different things, but when it comes down to it, we're all praying for the same

thing—*peace of mind*—something money can't buy. ML&R to you.

So many are facing Thanksgiving and Christmas with that Loved One missing, a vacant seat now sits at the dinner table. A limb has fallen from the family tree...you want to cry; the pain is like no other, and in time it will get better, but for now, just know that if any of them could whisper down to you, they'd say, "*Don't grieve for me, I'm no longer in pain. My worries are over. You wouldn't believe the spread that's laid out up here for Thanksgiving. Remember me with a smile, and someday soon we'll meet again, but until then, keep the traditions going, keep the family together, put a smile on your face, until I see you again. Happy Thanksgiving.*" ML&R

No one has the right to look down on anyone; only God stands that tall. ML&R

No one goes through life without problems, but if you do it right, you can make it through eternity without any. ML&R

Feel like you're facing a mountain? God parted the ocean; moving a little earth is no sweat. ML&R

"If you wait until you can do everything for everybody, instead of something for somebody, you'll end up doing nothing for nobody."

~ Malcom Bane

No disrespect intended to anyone, but just dressing up and going to church may not be enough; there comes a time the coat and tie has to come off and the jeans and boots put on for one to walk into the pits of Hell and drag out a Brother. Sometimes God needs our help just like we need His. ML&R

If you woke up this morning with no worries or cares, no pain, everything in your life is just beautiful, congratulations …you did it right while living on earth, you made it to Heaven. ML&R

God gave us two ears and one tongue. Maybe He was telling some of us we need to listen twice as much as we speak. ML&R

Going to church doesn't mean You'll never have problems. On any given Sunday, in any given church, there is at least one broken heart sitting on every pew...a good choice over a bar stool. ML&R

Everywhere we look, people are having problems: money, health, addictions, betrayals. Not one of us can escape them. Sooner or later, we all face something in our lives that will knock us to our knees, but that's not always a bad thing. While you're down there, look up and buy your ticket to the place where worry doesn't exist. They call it Heaven. ML&R

Listen up, guys, there's someone out there pretending to be your friend. He'll party with you, help you drink your booze, take a toke with you, may even sit beside you when you put that needle in your arm. He'll smile and tell you what a great world this is, while all the time he's taking it away from you. He's a salesman, my friends. He can talk you into going down that road not caring if you ever get back. Who is this man, you ask?

They call him the Devil. He's a lying piece of crap who will turn on you in a heartbeat. Serve him and he will betray you, take you all the way to the bottom, and look up—there he stands laughing at you. Don't run with a loser, my brothers. Get to know this man they call Jesus.

It won't make you weak; it'll just show that you're smart enough to run with someone that will always have your back, and not a punk that will lead you into a fight, then turn and run. ML&R

Sometimes it gets to the point where you just have to look up and say, "God, I can't do this alone, I need Your help." That doesn't make you weak. It just shows you're strong enough to call for backup. ML&R

We have problems we can't solve, so we do as they say, "Give them to Jesus"; then they seem to get worse, so we go back and get them. We couldn't handle them the first time, why do we think we can now? Be cool, give it time...don't be an Indian giver. Everything will work out in time.

Sitting on the balcony at 3:30 a.m., staring at the ocean and thinking God once told the sea to part and it did, and that makes Him big enough to take care of anything you or I can throw at Him. ML&R

Often I read a FB post and smile, sometimes shake my head, and sometimes come back and run my mouth. To the guy that posted "Running with the Devil on the

Highway to Hell, going to see my friends." Dude, I don't know if you're just trying to be cute or just plain stupid...get out there and hook up with the Devil, he'll take you on a ride you'll never forget. He has a way of making you feel ten feet tall and bullet proof. He'll walk with you into that bar, sit right beside you while you kick back a few, fill your chest with pride as you fire off that bike or crank that car.

What he won't tell you is that five miles up the road, he's gonna take your best friend. He won't show you the wife at home packing her bags because she's had enough of your nonsense, and he sure won't let you see those kids crying in bed wondering what tomorrow will bring. He has a way of making you feel like some kind of rock star until the Man Upstairs says *it's time*; now the Devil drops you off like the punk he really is, now you're riding solo, on that Highway To Hell...Take another route, Blood, you really don't want to run that road. ML&R

So many waking up to so many problems, thank goodness there is a God. It takes some prayers longer to get answered, not because God is not real; He's just making sure we are. ML&R

Sometimes God rocks our world just to remind us who's still in control. ML&R

Sometimes you just have to turn your problems over to God and get out of the way. He can move a lot faster when He's not having to work over your shoulder. ML&R

God took the time to wake you up this morning, guess that means He sees better things ahead. ML&R

Get out there and make a difference in someone's life. Remember God uses ordinary people to do extraordinary things. ML&R

Do things right; eternity is a long time to think about the things you did wrong. ML&R

When you pray, don't rush things, just lay back and wait for God's timing. It's better to wait and have things fall into place than rush and have them fall apart. ML&R

They say life is all about who you know, so is death. ML&R

Maybe your world is turned upside down because God is trying to get you to stand right side up. ML&R

Sometimes life gets so messed up we can't find the words to pray, but maybe it's better to have a heart without words than words without a heart. ML&R

If we could only see tomorrow, we'd probably have a better today. Don't worry, Jesus is already there. ML&R

While you're climbing a hill this morning, some are staring at a mountain. Always know that things could be worse. Rather than complain or worry, look up and thank God they're not. ML&R

If only we could forget our problems as fast as we forget our blessings. ML&R

"The longer you live, the more friends you'll bury," my Dad always told me, and as usual he was right...seems like when another one leaves, the ones that are gone come back to visit...I'm old, it won't ever get any easier; Death has no age; each day you stare it in the face. You're preaching your own funeral with each breath you take. You know there's a God, and you're thinking *"One day I'll change my ways."* Trust me, I know too many that didn't get that chance; their *"One day"* came too late.

I don't mean to come across like I'm preaching to you, man, I'm just *me*. Most of you will never see the things I've seen in life, or walk the road I walked. God smiled down on me for some reason while pulling the trigger on others. One day we're all going to have to look The Man in the eye, being a Bad Azz ain't going to be real cool right then...I've got this crazy feeling that I'm talking to someone out there, maybe I'm just talking to myself; either way it's something to think about. Sometimes tomorrow never comes, and yes, my friend, there is a Hell. Sunday morning coming down...ML&R

Stick with God in the good times; you wanted to hang with him in the bad. ML&R

GUILT: a pain that eats at your very soul...*If only I had done this or not done that*, a question you ask yourself for years. People tell you to put it behind you, that God

forgives; He has, but you can't. You look around and see lives you changed, the heartaches you caused, you tell the ones you can "I'm sorry," too late to tell others.

Being cool, running in the fast lane, living that Bad Boy image, thinking only of yourself, is NOT where it's at. One day you have to pay the tab, and when you look at the cost, you might just think it wasn't worth it. ML&R

Never think God has forgotten you, maybe He just put you on hold. He knows what you're going through...He's waiting to see what you're made of, teaching you to trust. You can bet He's got Your back, never fear. ML&R

Last night should teach us a lesson. We went to bed with the storm raging, only to wake this morning and the winds calmed. We're not to worry; God stays up all night. ML&R

When you go to bed tonight say a prayer, you don't even have to call a name, God knows we all need them. ML&R

Never get so self-righteous that you think you have the right to judge others. We'll all be judged someday, but I don't think God will turn to you and ask "What do *you* think?" ML&R

The only difference between saints and sinners is that every saint has a past and every sinner has a future!

Don't lose hope. When you are down to nothing, God is up to something.

Never think believing in God makes you weak, it's saying "I'm Stronger than the Devil." ML&R

If you think you're too good to speak to a drug addict or hug a homeless person, are you good enough to get into Heaven? Think about it. ML&R

Each of us awoke this morning with different problems but with the same Solution... God. There comes a time you have to change. God doesn't keep giving second chances to make the same mistake...ML&R

If God has your back against the wall, maybe he's just trying to get you to face him. ML&R

Getting right with The Man doesn't mean, *"OK, I've got my ticket bought, now I can relax."* if this place "Heaven" is what they tell me it is, I'd kinda like for my Brothers and Sisters to go with me...maybe you should too. ML&R

Next time you start to wonder if prayers get answered, think of the things you have now that you once prayed for. ML&R

There won't be a soul walking around Heaven carrying a grudge; maybe you'd better drop yours. ML&R

Rather than going to God everyday with a mouthful of *give me's*, maybe you need to make room and spit out a few *Thank You's*... ML&R

You don't have to jump benches or sit on the front row in church to be a Christian. Yesterday I talked to a biker

that most would distance themselves from, and he shared his beliefs and intentions. Don't ever judge a man by his appearance, lots of us are out here working undercover. ML&R

I pray I don't offend anyone, but this is really bothering me...I've got a long way to go, but I'm changing, and I see people who have been on the Dark Side, and they want to change also. I tell them to find a church, and too many times, I'm hearing "I don't own a suit," "I've been in jail, they wouldn't want me there."

Some people feel like they're not good enough to go to church. There's something wrong with this picture. Is any one of us better than another? We all sin, just in different ways. God loves us all...right? These are the people who need help. Come out of your Comfort Zone. Maybe it's time you 'walk among thieves'. ML&R

Think it's suppose to be in the low 40's tomorrow, so when you see a motorcycle on the road, don't be thinking *who is that Idiot?* I'll tell you who it is! It's my Brothers and Sisters making sure kids have Christmas...people who don't just think about helping others, they care enough to do something about it. They're good people, and I'm thinking if Jesus was here, He'd be riding with us. ML&R

Picture by Shirley McGuire Bradley

Putting things in God's hands doesn't mean He's going to walk in and pay your power bill or make your car payment...it means He's going to give you the good health to get a job and do it yourself. ML&R

Life Lessons

If you'll work half as hard in your young age being good to people and making friends as you do trying to make a dollar, you'll be twice as rich when you get older. ML&R

It doesn't matter if they don't have two quarters to rub together, never look down on anyone. Their dignity may be all they have left. ML&R

Always stand by your Brother or Sister, hold them up when they can't stand on their own. Heck, we're just walking each other home, anyway. ML&R

Don't sit there in Your $500 suit, drinking high dollar booze and putting someone down for drinking too much at a local bar...I'm thinking a drunk is a drunk, the place has nothing to do with it.

No need to worry...the hardest battles you'll ever face in life are the ones you didn't see coming.

Ten years from now, make sure you can look back at your life and say you chose it, not settled for it.

No one deserves 2nd best...better to aim high and miss than to aim low and hit. ML&R

It's not about how many mountains you face in life, it's how you climb them. ML&R

Everything happens for a reason. Often not getting what we ask for is a big stroke of luck. ML&R

If you dance with drugs long enough, they'll eventually take you to bed with them. ML&R

Life doesn't get better by chance; often you have to change. ML&R

Never give up! When something bad happens, usually something good comes of it. ML&R

No matter what you're going through, it won't last. Everything comes to pass, and that includes your troubles. ML&R

Everyone makes mistakes. We were put here to be real, not perfect. ML&R

Worry is just part of the game...we go through a little stress just before success. Give it time. ML&R

In life, it always helps to look up, but there comes a time you have to grow up. ML&R

May the worry you wake up with this morning be just an afterthought when you hit the bed tonight. ML&R

Always think before you act; every choice you make has consequences. You are today what you decided yesterday to become. ML&R

"Never be afraid to try anything. Remember the Ark was built by amateurs while the Titanic was built by professionals."

~ Unknown

Be yourself. Sheep run in herds, but eagles fly alone.

Better to be criticized by a wise man than to be praised by a fool.

~ Ecclesiastes 5:7

One thing you can give and still keep is your word.

"Be careful who you step on while climbing the ladder of success, you could need their help coming back down."

~ Wilson Mizner

If we learn from our mistakes, I should be a genius by now!

Anger is just one letter short of danger.

The easiest way to keep a secret is without help.

If they gossip with you, they'll gossip about you.

You haven't lost if you tried and failed. You've lost if you fail and give up.

If you dislike me, remember, it's mind over matter. I don't mind and you don't matter.

Don't make a reputation you'll have to live down or run away from later.

Never trade the thrills of living for the security of existence.

Live your life like you bank: yesterday is a cancelled check, tomorrow is a promissory note, today is cash!

Always forgive your enemies, but never forget their names.

The nice part of living in a small town is that when I don't know what I'm doing, someone else does.

Don't worry about life; you're not going to survive it anyway.

Dream as if you will live forever, live as if you will die today.

Life has its ups and downs...if you're down this morning, guess what, your next move is up. ML&R

If they start off by saying "they told me not to say anything, *but,* " you'd better be careful what you say in return. They just showed you who you're talking to. ML&R

Did you ever think maybe God didn't wake you up today for your sake, but for someone else's? Help somebody if you can. ML&R

Everyone makes mistakes, and you guys that won't let them forget it are living proof. ML&R

Never show anyone so much respect that it causes you to lose yours...sometimes your dignity is all you have left. ML&R

Be careful what you say to family and friends today, it could be the last thing they'll ever hear. ML&R

If You're not willing to work for it, what makes you think you deserve it ? Just thinkin...

Sometimes the people you think have it all together are the ones falling apart. Never judge a book by it's cover. ML&R

If you know a person is going through a difficult time in their life, why don't you try talking to them instead of talking about them...just shows what you're made of. ML&R

Be careful who you vent to...a listening ear often turns into a running mouth. ML&R

Two things that define you as a person: your patience when you have nothing and your attitude when you have everything. ML&R

You can knock a person down with a 2x4, and in a few moments, hopefully, they'll get back up. Knock a person down with your tongue and it could take a lifetime. Even when we were babies, God let us think before we learned to talk. ML&R

Some people are Legends in their own mind...you don't build a reputation on what you thought about doing. ML&R

So many people, so many problems...Keep looking up, miracles fall out of Heaven...hope you catch yours today.

Too often the people with the most to hide are the first to judge. ML&R

Sometimes I wonder if some of the people we'd take a bullet for would ever attend our funeral.

When someone tells you that you're doing wrong, it's not always them judging you; it just might be because they love you. ML&R

Never judge a person by what someone else told you. ML&R

Live today so when someone goes to bed tonight they're glad you did. ML&R

Don't wake up stressing; God just gave you a blessing...make the most of it. ML&R

The way people treat you is a reflection of who they are, not who you are. ML&R

Give a smile, give your time, give someone your hand, give a complement, give forgiveness, give a hug, and most of all, give thanks. ML&R

Never take away someone's hope, it may be all they have left. ML&R

Never judge a person.....Some of us haven't quite gotten to where we're going, but we'll never go back to where we've been. ML&R to Ya

Life has it's ups and downs, and no one remembers the nights they got a good night's sleep...those sleepless nights are the ones that you'll remember. ML&R

In life you can either get attention or respect...Go for the respect, Youngbloods, it lasts longer. ML&R

So often we bring worry on ourselves. Even if we mean well, maybe we should stay out of other people's business 'til we're invited in. ML&R

When you've finally climbed to the top of the mountain, never take your eyes off the people still in the valley. They may be the very ones that catch you if you slip and fall. ML&R

Some on FB ask for prayers one day, then cuss and rant the next; that's like borrowing money and not paying it back...I don't think that's the way it works. ML&R

Sometimes life will knock us lower than we've ever been, just so we can learn to stand taller than we ever have. ML&R

What would you do differently today if you knew you were going to check out of this world at midnight tonight? You know your weak points; why not start working on them now and get ahead of the game. ML&R

As you drink your coffee this morning, someone is being hooked up to an IV. As you get into your car, someone is being loaded into an ambulance. As you walk into your job, someone is making funeral arrangements. Hope your morning just got better. ML&R

I know four, maybe you know more, that this time last Sunday, didn't have a clue they wouldn't be here today. We think we're going to live forever, but in reality this day could be our last. Life is precious, but there is a hereafter, where you'll spend it is up to you...Love the

people around you, it's what they'll remember when you're gone. ML&R

Never feel beneath or inferior to anyone. They may dress better than you or have a nicer house, but always remember they have diarrhea just like the rest of us...ML&R

Life is not about what you take when you leave this world behind you, it's what you leave behind you when you go. ML&R

The most important lessons in life aren't learned in school. You learn them from a hungry stomach, an empty pocket, and a broken heart...Life is not for sissies. ML&R

In a couple of day it'll be Thanksgiving. Have you ever thought what it would be like to spend it alone? You wake up with an empty feeling in your gut; you walk through the house seeing nothing but four bare walls. Families gathering across the street, while past memories flood your mind. You open a can of pork and beans while others carve the turkey. The walls start closing in, so you go for a ride, but everywhere you look, cars fill the driveway, kids are playing in the yard, people are hanging with family.

It's a tough day, Everyone giving thanks while you're asking for forgiveness. This year, give someone a reason to be thankful, just a phone call or maybe a short visit. You might miss part of the football game, but you'll make a memory someone will take to their grave. ML&R

As I reach the end of my journey on Hwy #2015, I look over my shoulder and I see the good days and I see the bad...days I smiled at a newborn and days I laid a friend to rest.. .days I wanted to hug everyone and days I wanted to choke a few...mornings I couldn't wait to get out of bed and mornings I had to ask God for help just to get up...days the road was so smooth I just kicked back and smiled, and some so rough I had to hang on for dear life.

We all traveled the same road, just at different times, and we made it. As I approach the intersection of Hwy #2016, I can't help but wonder what's ahead, but then I look around and see my family, my brothers and sisters riding with me; I look up and see God looking down and I know I'm not alone. We'll run this road together, help each other along the way. Kickstands up, it's going to be a good ride. ML&R

Listen up, Youngbloods: If you haven't found out by now, the world is not all peaches and cream. Fact of the matter, at times it can be a mean and nasty place, and it can knock you to your knees and keep you there if you let it. I don't care how badass you think you are, the world can hit harder. You have to learn to take the punches and keep rolling. Don't ever give up or blame others saying it's his or her fault you're where you are. That's a coward's way out, and you're better than that. ML&R

When I was young and wild and my Dad was still alive, He use to tell me " Boy, you don't believe cow horns will hook." Youngbloods, after many years of research, I'm here to tell you they will...ML&R

When life goes south, the last thing you should worry about is *what will other people think*. There's not a person here that doesn't have something going on in their life that they're having to deal with. No one is perfect. Every person, every family has their problems.

Maybe instead of talking about them, you should pray for them. Use your words wisely and send them up to God. Don't spread them to your neighbor. No person or family escapes troubles or hard times unless they've already died and gone to Heaven, and I figure they have better things to do up there than read Facebook...Don't throw stones; you never know when someone is holding the rock that could shatter Your glass house. ML&R

Class reunions can be an intimidating experience. Sitting in the car before going in, I got scared...should I be here? What will people think? Maybe I should have shaved and gotten a haircut. Naw, I am what I am, lets do this. Walking in the door, I could see people looking, even read one person's lips, " There's Eddie Jolley." I'm out of my zone; instead of feeling like The Man, I'm feeling inferior...the people there weren't doing it, they were great; it was me putting me down. I'm seeing the ones that had it together even in high school, like one guy who said "I don't think we had any classes together" I'm thinking, *no, you were going to college, I was just trying to get through thinking I'd go to work or take a visit to Vietnam.*

I sit at the table and look around; I see the cheerleaders, the guys that played ball, where were the ones that hung with me in the smoking hall? We all took different roads; last night we came back together, some with scars on our bodies, some with scars on our souls. We're no longer kids, the hair has turned gray; we have kids and grandkids, we did it our way...To everyone there, it was an honor to have known you...The class of 1965 had it's dreams, we just didn't know how complicated it got after we turned 18. ML&R to each of you.

As I stopped in to pick up our carry-out for dinner tonight, I noticed a guy sitting leaning against the building. I could tell by his looks he was probably down on his luck...As I walked by and said hello, he responded with a "Hi", never asked for a thing, just sat and dropped his head. Coming out the door with order in my hand, I walked over and asked if he was OK. A conversation started; it's amazing how much you can learn from a person in just a few minutes. Yeah, he was strung out, nowhere to live, family long gone, hadn't eaten since yesterday.

Here goes my rant: to the man and lady that were coming in as we talked, I just want you to know he heard you, I heard you, *"Sorry bum,"* you said as you walked by. Dude, it's people like you that have made the world the way it is today. He did nothing to you, never asked you for a dime, but what you don't know is he saved you from an azz-kicking, because when I stood up I was coming for you, he's the one that said "let it go, It's ok."

Maybe I'm a hypocrite; I tell you to love one another, but some really make it hard. Please, nobody deserves to be disrespected, keep your comments to yourself. They hear, they hurt...they're someone's husband, son

72

or brother, they're people. I gave him my dinner; God forgive me, I hope yours made you sick.

Nothing in the world can screw up your day like your own thoughts.

Had several comments last week about me preaching at the Blessing of the Bikes...Come on, guys, that was Eddie Jolley, nothing close to a preacher. I like to think of it as a Older Brother talking to his Younger Brothers and Sisters, warning them of the traps this old world has set for them. Yeah, I tell 'em to get right with the Man, and if that makes me weak, well that's ok. You see, I've lived long enough to have run both roads and I think I'd rather go to Heaven humbled than to ride into Hell a badass...Have a Good Day and take care of the ones you love. ML&R

When life knocks you down, you can lie there and feel sorry for yourself, or you can jump back up and prove yourself. ML&R

When life knocks you down, you can lie there and feel sorry for yourself, or you can jump back up and prove yourself. ML&R

When life knocks you down, you can lie there and feel sorry for yourself, or you can jump back up and prove yourself. ML&R

Photograph by David Staley

Weekends... While some are happy-go-lucky, others are sick, depressed, feeling like life has knocked them to their knees. Ride it out, guys. God loves us all the same and He has no favorites; your time will come. ML&R

I post a lot about life, not because I'm smarter than you, just because I've seen more of it than most. I'd never try to tell you what to do, but I do try to warn you what not to do. Some say I even preach at times. Lord knows I'm far from that. Most preachers stand in the pulpit and tell you about sin, things they learn in the Good Book; sometimes I tell you things because I learned it in Life. I've lived it, seen things none of you ever want to see, been places none of you ever want to go, always searching for that next high, that next rush, that I called happiness.

I tried to find it in cars, motorcycles, bars, behind a set of drums, even the women. The cars caused me to bury some of my best friends, the bikes took me through Hell, the bars destroyed some of my friends, the drums took me away from my home and family; the women, especially one, I wish she could hear me say "I'm sorry."

Listen up, guys, we're all trying to find happiness and we do, a little at a time, but it seems like it doesn't last, so we keep looking 'til eventually you figure it out: it's right here under our noses: our families, our health, our friends, and last but not least, the Man Upstairs.

You have to figure out you're not The Man. No family is perfect, and friends will let you down. All prayers don't always get answered, but you never give up on any of the above. A time will come when you have to look up and say "God, I did it my way and it didn't work. I just thought I knew it all, but I need a hand to hold, maybe just something to believe in... ML&R

Wanna lighten that heavy load you're carrying around? Knock that chip off your shoulder. ML&R

There comes a time when you have to think about the people that are holding you down and the ones that are holding you up. Separate them and move on with your life. ML&R

You gotta be real in life. Always be yourself; don't put on a show. You are who you are and you are what you are. People see through you...when it's all said and done, when we've taken our last ride, I want people to remember my story as fact, not fiction.

Failure doesn't mean you have wasted your life, it just means you have a reason to start over. ML&R

Never go in debt trying to keep up with the Joneses; about the time you catch them, they'll refinance...sometimes that credit card can be a gift from Hell.

So many running the wrong road, thinking "I have the rest of my life to make things right." True story: Three of us got on motorcycles one night, within 15 minutes, one lived the rest of his life...Think about it, my young brothers.

Life gets easier once you quit letting other people's actions hit you between your eyes and start letting them go over your head.

Life isn't the kind of journey that comes with a map. There are times we have to follow our hearts and make the best decisions we can, the best way we know how. At times the road is straight, and other times it is rough and bumpy, but along the way, we learn a lot about ourselves, and even when we don't know exactly where it will end, we know we'll arrive the same way we started...with family and friends.

Take a few shots, the party gets wilder; pack your nose, the world gets brighter; pop a few pills, you dull the pain; take a hit, you can roll for days...just a few billboard signs you'll see as you travel that Highway to Hell...take the next exit, My Friends. ML&R To Ya

Most of us have been there...we needed a friend. No, we didn't want to borrow your money, didn't even want someone to party with; we just need someone to *listen*. Don't ever get too busy in life that you don't have time for a friend; someday the shoe may be on the other foot. ML&R

There comes a times in life when you just have to stop playing defense and realize everyone is not out to get you. Learn to let a few things go over your head, not because you're small, but because you're too big to put up with their nonsense. ML&R

Life has it's ups and downs, the good and the bad, it's no different for any of us. Today we may have a smile on our face, only to have tears streaming down it tomorrow. We're all on the same ride, just different roads, same destination. Where we spend it is up to us.

Do it Right, Guys, I'd kinda like to hang with all of you forever. ML&R

If anyone ever told you life was easy, they lied...It's a fight, one battle after another, with a few rest stops in between. Sometimes you have to reach down in your soul and pull something out that you didn't know was there...that's how you find out what you're made of...today might be a good day to go searching.

A lot of us have spent a holiday alone, and I for one will tell you it is the most depressing day you'll ever experience. If you know someone that has lost a loved one, going through a divorce, or just old and outlived their family, what's two more feet under your table gonna hurt? Why not invite them over...when they hit their knees that night they'll have something to be thankful for...YOU. ML&R

I'm about to lay something heavy on you, if you can't handle it you might need to move on...New Year's Eve is next week, probably the party night of the year. Yeah, I've played and been to more than most of you. Before you drink and drive, let me tell you what can happen, because I've seen it up close and personal twice in my life...

Drink gives you courage: *Nah, I can do this, it won't happen to me*...then from nowhere, BANG! it happens; car flipping, motorcycle flying through the air, bodies twisted, blood flowing, a Brother begging " please don't let me die." You want to run, pretend it's not happening, but you can't leave him, so you hold his head, he closes his eyes...he's gone.

By now cars are stopping, red lights and blue lights everywhere. You see a wife, Mom and Dad, turn into zombies right before your eyes. You go to the funeral home, stand over a Brother, tears fall on him. You walk out the door, but he goes with you; he wakes you during the night asking, "Why didn't you stop me?"

Party if you must, but for God's sake and yours, get a designated driver, hire a taxi, look out for your Brothers and Sisters, don't let them leave drunk. I promise you'll be glad you did. ML&R

Never try to ruin someone's life with a lie when yours could probably be destroyed with the truth. ML&R

Never be jealous or envious of anything another person has; you don't know how many nights they lie in bed wondering how they're going to keep it...Keep it simple and you'll sleep better. ML&R to Ya

25 years from now you're married, have kids, doing the right thing. One thing's gonna hang with you—your reputation! Some will let you live it down, too many won't. Maybe you were a fighter, a boozer, did a few drugs, maybe you slept around. My young Brothers and Sisters, make the right choices now; you're gonna have to live with them for the rest of your life. People may forgive but they don't forget. ML&R I give you.

Why would anyone call you an addict? Just because you wake each morning wondering where you're gonna score those pills? Maybe everyone smokes a joint before breakfast, and those 4 or 5 shots you have at night are just to help you rest, and that meth pipe you carry around is just a conversation piece. No, you're not an addict. Most of them have already lost their family and home; they're way ahead of you...you're just on your way. ML&R

Enjoy life...there is an expiration date.

Don't waste your time trying to impress other people. being a fake takes too much time, while being real takes no effort at all. ML&R

Too often, we get life all screwed up. We look at the people around us that actually love us and pay them no attention, while trying our best to please people that someday won't make a crap. Don't wait to wake up one day when it's too late and say, *"What was I thinking?* ML&R

Stop thinking you're stuck in your situation forever. You may feel like your heart will never heal, or you're never going to get out of the problem you're facing, but don't confuse a season for a lifetime. Every hardship has an expiration date. You will grow, life will change, and things always work out. ML&R

I ran through life in the Fast Lane; thinkin' now I should have taken the Scenic Route...

Don't expect people to look you in the eye if you're looking down on them.

A bad thing about following the herd: you have to watch where you step

No matter how high you climb in life, never forget where you came from and who helped put you there.

If you want something to be grateful for, check your pulse!

"What most people need to learn in life is how to love people and use things instead of using people and loving things."

~ Unknown.

Bad habits are like a comfortable bed—easy to get into, hard to get out of.

If I had a Brother needing money, I could loan him a buck; needed somewhere to stay, show him a bed; getting his butt kicked, jump in beside him, but when his heart is broken, that's a tough one. When you hit your knees tonight keep a Brother in your prayers; I sure have him in mine. ML&R

One day your life will flash before your eyes; make sure it's worth watching.

Just because they won't come up to your standards, don't fall to theirs.

Stand up for your country. If you've never had a leader that made you a little nervous, you've never had much of a leader. ML&R

You have to stay strong, never give up. So many times I thought my world was falling apart, when it was actually falling together. ML&R

Too often I guess I speak of the past, but you have to realize there's more behind me than there is in front of me. Yesterday was a prime example. With a back telling me *"no"* but a heart saying *"yes,"* I attended a benefit the CCIB was putting on for the kids. Riding in and getting hugs and handshakes kinda makes the pain and worries go away. Little did I know when we pulled out that God was going to put me in a "time coma."

Running handlebar to handlebar with a friend I hadn't ridden with in 25 years, the memories started filling my brain, remembering so many of what we once thought were the good times. Looking ahead and seeing bikes in front, looking in the mirror and seeing them behind, took me back another 20 years, remembering the ones that were there, but now gone. Making a stop at a club and walking in for the first time in 45 years, looking at a stage, and thinking of the nights you stood on it, and thinking of the guys that are now making music in Heaven.

We make our memories and they bring a smile to our faces, but with some of those great times, we now see they were tearing our world apart, mistakes made, lives shattered, lives lost, all for the sake of a good time. With one foot in the grave, I look back and think *if only I had put God and family ahead of this other stuff how would my life been different?* I guess I'll never know, but you guys are young, you still have the time to find out...do it right. ML&R

Don't spend your time wishing things were better; something could happen to make you see they weren't really that bad. ML&R

Hard times are often blessings in disguise. Let go and let life build you. No matter how much it hurts, hold your head up and keep going. This is an important lesson when you're having a bad day, a bad month, or a crappy year. Truth be told, sometimes the hardest lessons to learn are the ones you need the most. Your past was never a mistake if you learned from it, so take all those crazy experiences and lessons and place them in a box and label them *Thank You*. ML&R

People waking up this morning headed to the hospital, some looking for a job, some even getting ready to bury a loved one, and all you have to do is go to work. Always something to be thankful for, you got lucky today. ML&R

Learn to be content with what you have. Better to do without than to go broke trying to look rich. ML&R

The next time you start to take someone for granted, imagine your life without them. ML&R

Too often bad things happen, but to some, it's not bad enough, so they add a twist to it to make it sound better. Listen up, if you just heard it with your ears and haven't seen it with your eyes, keep your mouth shut and your fingers off the keyboard. There's always a family going through Hell. It's called *respect.*

The ones that judge will never understand, and those that understand will never judge. ML&R

It's just how life is: many people don't deserve what they get, and many don't get what they deserve. ML&R

Some people are waking up on vacation, some getting ready to bury loved ones; some are in the hospital, whole some are just wondering how they're going to pay their bills. I've lived through each of these mornings; hang in there and one day you'll look back and say "I did too." ML&R

There are millions and millions of people in the world; why let just one control your life? ML&R

Rather than complaining about it being Monday and you having to go to work, be thankful...realize how many out there are sick or disabled or have lost their job and are out looking this morning? Look up and be grateful; God could turn your complaint into another person's blessing. ML&R

Don't get confused in life.. It's God #1, family #2, and that motorcycle or car #3...Don't get turned around about that, or you could live to regret it. ML&R

There comes a time when you have to start thinking about yourself and realize the people you're thinking about the most are the ones thinking about you the least...don't let yourself die worrying about the way others live. ML&R

While you sit in a warm house, someone is homeless and cold. As you eat dinner, someone is going to sleep hungry. As you look at your family, someone just buried one today. Life is really not that bad, is it? ML&R

Always remember when going through life, you can be either a Giver or a Taker. The Taker will eat better, but the Giver will sleep better. ML&R

Photograph by Ruby Briscoe Harris

If I'm lucky enough to live 3 more weeks, I'll be 70 years old, the guy that was always told he'd never see 21.

I tell you things I've done, not to brag, but to try and warn you. Mama tried to warn me and I didn't listen. She took me to Sunday school, taught me about The Man, but somewhere along the line I decided I no longer needed Him. I was running hard and fast, thinking of no one but myself. Some of the things we saw should have turned us, but I think it just made us harder. We were losing the love of good decent women, burying our brothers, and worst of all, we were losing our souls.

If I could look each of you in the eye, I'd tell you to slow it down, love your family, stay away from the dope and booze, never take life for granted, and the Most Important Thing, don't forget there is a God. Some of us Ole Timers are starting to slow down, not because we want to, but Nature has a way of doing it for us. So the next time you see that old dude with scars on his body, walking with a limp, pointing you in another direction, trust him. He's not trying to be a Smart Azz; he opened the road for you 50 years ago, and he's just trying to keep you on the right one...getting lost can be hell. ML&R

Relationships

So, you don't like dating single moms because you think they're too desperate? Most single moms run their own home, pay their own bills, take care of the kids while sometimes working two jobs. In all reality, you should be happy she has time for your stupid azz in her life at all. ML&R to the working single moms, you're the American Bad Azz.

Sometimes you just have to move on. Some will say "You're not what I thought you were." Look them in the eye and say "You're Right, I'm Better." ML&R

When people start treating you like they no longer care, believe them. ML&R

Ladies, don't jump in bed with a guy the first time you meet him. You may hurt his feelings but you just got his respect. ML&R

In every successful relationship the man always has the last word: *"Yes, Dear."*

Life has a way of making you look back to the ones who loved you, the ones who really cared, who are now gone. You'll remember the good times, but wonder about the bad: *Did I cause them grief, did I cause them to worry? Maybe they'd have been better off had I not been around.* You know, it's not always about you. When someone loves you, that's pretty special. Only a few actually do, and don't hurt them, don't fight, because one day they'll be gone and you could be here on a Sunday morning wishing you had one more chance to do it right. ML&R

Don't start your day thinking of the ones tearing you apart; think of the ones holding you together. ML&R

Take people for better or for worse; just never take them for granted. ML&R

For men who think a woman's place is in the kitchen, just remember that's where the knives are kept!

So many searching for that one person to change their life when all they have to do is look in the mirror. ML&R

"Men who don't understand women fall into two groups: Bachelors and Husbands."

~ Daniel Tosh

Never change who you are just to please someone else...that's lying to two people. ML&R

"The best way to remember your wife's birthday is to forget it once."

~ E. Joseph Cossman

It's bad to lose someone you love, but it's worse if you lose yourself trying to stay with them. ML&R

"A foolish man tells a woman to stop talking, but a wise man tells her that her mouth is beautiful when her lips are closed."

~ Robert Bloch

Treat your wife the way you'd want your daughter to be treated. ML&R

Hang tight, you'll get over it. It's better to lose a lover than love a loser. ML&R

Lady, think about it: this dude is going to leave his wife and small kid to move in with you and take care of you and yours? Call me, I have a beach front home for sale in Asheville, cheap...SMH

So many searching for that one person to change their life, when all they have to do is look in the mirror. ML&R

Never lie to someone who trusts you, and never trust someone who lies to you.

It's better to tell the truth, even if you make them cry, than to tell a lie and make them smile. ML&R

Respect yourself enough to say, "I deserve peace," and walk away from people or things that stop you from having it. ML&R

So many lives changed, so many regrets just because of lack of communication.

Next time you start complaining about your baby's daddy, remember you picked him.

Some people are heaven-sent, while others are running errands for the Devil...know the difference. ML&R

There comes a time you have to stop trying to change a person who doesn't want to change...stop giving chances to someone who takes advantage of your forgiveness. Stop running back to where your heart ran from. Stop trusting their words and ignoring their actions. Stop breaking your own heart. ML&R

ML&R

Photo by Kimberly Pruett Mullinax